www.BeirBuaPress.com

(Un)Natural Elements

by

Laura Besley

Published by Beir Bua Press

ISBN: 978-1-914972-19-5

Copyright © 2021 by Laura Besley

All rights reserved.

No part of this publication may be reproduced, distributed, or transmitted in any form or by any means, including photocopying, recording, or other electronic or mechanical methods, without the prior written permission of the publisher, except in the case of brief quotations embodied in critical reviews and certain other noncommercial uses permitted by copyright law. For permission requests, contact the author, Laura Besley.

Beir Bua Press, Co. Tipperary, Ireland.

Typesetting / Layout, Cover Design: Michelle Moloney King Cover image: Michelle Moloney King

Ordering Information: For details, see www.BeirBuaPress.com

Published by Beir Bua Press

Printed in the UK

Our printer is certified as a B Corporation to measure our impact on the environment and help drive us to be even more conscious of our footprint.

Dedication

For readers and lovers of tiny tales.

Acknowledgments

The author would like to thank the following journals and competitions for previously publishing the following stories, in this form or similar, as:

Salt I – 'Bones and Skin' – Mythic Picnic V6
Salt III – 30 word stories
Skin I – 'Silenced' – Emerge Literary Journal
Sky I – 'Black(ness) Descends – Mythic Picnic V4
Soil I – 'Fade to Black' – Page & Spine
Stars I – 'Falling Star' – Ellipsis Nine
Stars II – 'Her Glorious Face' – 50 word stories
Steel I – 'Love at the Foot of the Mountain' – The Birdseed, issue 1.
Steel II – 'Hands, Born and Bred to Work' – 50-word stories
Stone I – 'Homecoming' – 101 Words
Stone II – Reflex fiction – winner 50-word story competition

Introduction

Firstly, I'd like to thank Michelle at Beir Bua Press - not only for publishing *(Un)Natural Elements* and for trusting my vision for this collection, but also for her dedication to experimental writing and running a press which makes publications like this one possible.

Many of these stories were written as tweet-length stories from daily prompts on Twitter under the hashtag: Very Short Story 365 (#vss365). After a few people kindly suggested I collate them, I decided to look at all the stories I had written to date and to my delight found myself able to see patterns and themes. There was also a strong use of nature within them and the idea to divide the collection into elements emerged organically.

Once the structure of nine elements was in place, I completed the collection with some longer stories - some of which have been previously published, whereas others are new.

To everyone reading this collection - thank you - and I sincerely hope you enjoy these tiny tales.

Salt

I

I see you looking. Yes, you. Staring even. Your slim hips perched on the bar stool trying to work us out: a good-looking middle-aged man, and me.

You hop down and sashay over to the table. Greg and I order steak and chips. 'Anything else?' you ask. 'No,' I say, snapping the menu shut, when what I really want to say is: Yes, I was a fucking catch once, you know.

It was after one of these anniversary dinners that I first cried during sex. Greg assured me that my extra weight and wrinkles didn't matter. Would never matter, until that last time when his eyes never quite met mine. No tears that night and dry ever since.

When the steak arrives, it's overcooked, drained of any succulence. I could send it back, but instead I moan, pretending it's the best steak I've ever had.

II

When your life falls apart, it's not the final crash that seals your fate.

No.

It's the cracks and splinters,

the gentle corrosions,

pieces smaller than grains of salt breaking off,

dispersing,

until one day you step back,

look,

and find it's damaged beyond repair.

III

Tangs of sea-salt air and vinegar-drenched chips lure me to my home town.

A charity shop window displays my mother's dinner service and I realise she's dead.

Overhead, gulls cry.

IV

Home early from work, I hear sounds coming from the living room. It's

my boyfriend – wanking.

He's nearing the end, so I go to the kitchen, sprinkle salt on the joint of

meat,

put it in the oven.

Later, I tiptoe my fingertips down his torso.

'Don't Bea,' he says. 'I'm tired.'

Fucker. I swig the dregs of wine from the bottle, the taste in my mouth

bitter.

V

BRIGHT WHITE LIGHT is all I know – reflecting off the salt flats, illuminating my childhood, my schooldays and holidays, my Christmases and birthdays, my friendships and family.

BRIGHT WHITE LIGHT is everywhere – trapped in the clouds above us and the salt below us, in our houses, our beds, in the kisses we give our lovers, in the lullabies we sing to our children. But the DARKNESS is creeping in.

BRIGHT WHITE LIGHT is fading. Like my parents before me and their parents before them, I thought I'd be the one who kept my sight, but I too have been robbed, my eyes deprived, dried out like the seas that once sat in this barren land, until finally I am left in total DARKNESS.

Sea

I

Thinking the sea soundproof, I wade into the waves, deeper and deeper, until I'm immersed – and scream.

A glitter of mermaids, their legs and sex sealed in scaly tails, swarm around me.

'Life on land is hard,' one says.

Another says, 'Come live with us. Be free.'

A merman glides by thrashing his huge tail. The mermaids swish their hair and suck in their stomachs.

Life is no different here, I think, and swim back to shore.

When I resurface, cliffs have crumbled covering soft sands with misshapen rocks.

I start walking home on my two legs, each step steadier.

II

The fog crept in unnoticed; clouded my thoughts, clenched my heart.

On the brink of disappearance, I wade in the sea shallows, a glint of me reemerging.

I will never know which force fought hardest, the saltwater or love for myself, but either way, the cloud is lifting.

III

I join the hunt for the missing girl. We comb through long grass, forage in the undergrowth, scour the beach.

One of the police dogs never leaves my side.

By dawn, the girl has not yet been found and I have killed the dog.

IV

When there are no more women to lie with men, seals are pulled onto shore.

Older generations show them how to keep house, keep trim, keep the men happy.

None of the babes birthed have legs and the mamas return to the roar of the sea, fattened cubs in tow.

V

'I want you to scatter my ashes at sea, Lizzie,' you said, your grip surprisingly strong. 'Promise me.'

'But you hate the water, Mum.'

'Only because I was scared. I don't need to be scared anymore.'

On a gentle spring day, I wade out and tip the tin.

Decide I can be brave, too.

Skin

I

It's everywhere. It's there when I close my eyes to go to sleep at night. It's in my dreams. It's the first thing I see when I wake up in the morning. It's stenciled onto my retina, overlaying all the good memories I have of my daughter. It's there when I recall her body with bruises in all the wrong places.

That smile is everywhere.

That it-wasn't-me smile; that I-know-people-in-high-places smile; that released-due-to-inconclusive-evidence smile.

The same smile I saw fade just before I cut it from his face.

At home, I pull down my daughter's childhood worry box and blow off the dust which curls and dances in the quiet of her room. I open the lid, and without looking at the faded notes in her child-like scrawl, put the smile inside. 'All gone,' I whisper, just like I always did, and put the box back on the shelf.

II

She draws darts on her waist,
hips and thighs,
reaches for the scissors,
and cuts away the excess flesh.
Bloodied and stitched,
she now fits into the dress he bought her.

At dinner,
her smile never falls,
unlike the blood that pools at her feet.

III

In nighttime hours,
our bodies forget
we still seek forgiveness
for words spilled from our daytime mouths.

We wake,
arms and legs entangled in warm sheets,
breath halted,
wondering if our bodies can heal
where our words
cannot.

IV

After her husband leaves for work, Asha runs a bath, fills it with spices.

The heat and smells remind her of home, long left and far away.

After, her skin shimmering and cooling, she scrubs the bath back to its cold drab state.

V

my skin

once tattooed

by the ink of

your love

is now stretched,

faded and

ugly.

My body is

left

covered

in nothing but

vandalism.

Sky

I

Every morning I tiptoe across the dew-damp garden and fill the bird feeder with seeds. Then I sit, fingers curled around my first coffee of the day, and wait.

'Haunted,' the neighbour said. 'That's how you bought it so quickly.' Paul and I laughed, oh how we laughed, sipping our chilled drinks on the sandstone patio.

Two months later he was killed. Hit by a bus. Gone.

'Instantly,' the paramedic said. 'Take some comfort in that.'

I rubbed my stomach, a new, but comforting, habit, but she decided she couldn't stay either.

One crow lands; big, black eyes watching me. Then another, and another, until the garden is awash with them. I would hate them, but they're all I have now.

II

I've tried setting Dad's pigeons free, but they always come back.

Out of love?

Loyalty?

Habit?

Today a wild pigeon lands on the roof. As I watch it, it seems to be beckoning me.

I spread my wings and we fly off together.

III

On our first date you gave me an origami rose.

After a year you proposed with an origami ring and we married in an origami church.

Together we built an origami house, had three origami children.

In the final folds of my life, when doctors cast down their origami eyes and shook their origami heads, you gave me origami wings, to be free of pain like an origami bird.

IV

I never name the child I birth, clawed and feathered, but put its beak to my breast, let it suckle once before opening the window and watching it take flight.

V

You crash land from the sky, colouring my heart and life petrichor.

Our bright burning love, which once kept you grounded, fades to wispy blue. I shower you in gifts of gold to weigh you down, but every day you float higher and higher.

One chilly winter morning I wake and you are gone. I imagine you drifting amongst the clouds – happier; where you belong.

Snow

I

My legs know the way, trudging my boots through compacted snow, as my mind wanders.

Back to hot chocolates after school, you helping me with my homework; back to nursing mum, you showing me how; back to dressing in black, you holding my hand all day; back to that fight after Billy Caulfield told me you weren't my real dad, you telling me it didn't matter. Back to me leaving.

You were wrong. It did matter, still matters, more than words can convey.

I see the smoke snaking out of the squat chimney, push the gate open, knowing I'm home.

II

June snow; a miracle.

Maybe God's open to prayers today. I beg him to reverse time, make the driver see your blood-red tricycle.

My eyes open; not snow, but blossom.

*

III

I unravel a cloud in the night sky.

Memories of you and me spill out in a flurry of snow and ice, scattering far and wide.

In the morning, they coat the grass, the leaves, the trees.

By lunchtime the sun has melted them away, like they never even existed.

IV

Words sting like sleet on skin until I'm numb. My body breaks, limbs and fingers snap off.

Segmentation complete, you sweep me into a corner where I must rebuild myself again.

*

V

On his way to school, Jack saw a snowman. Stomach rumbling, he ate the carrot nose, then the coal eyes and finally the stones that made the smile.

Although he was cold, Jack left the scarf, retying the length of it into a neat Windsor knot.

Every morning thereafter, the snowman waited for Jack to pass, a tub of food tucked beside his tubby tummy.

Soil

I

'Start with a plant,' my therapist said. 'Something easy and uncomplicated. Show it love, talk to it, allow it to love you back.'

I huffed and puffed in the session, but I bought a plant from the supermarket. A gerbera. Pale pink. Couldn't cope with one of those brightly-coloured ones. I put it in the kitchen which gave me a reason to get out of bed every morning. I watered it, talked to it, learned to love it.

But the plant died.

My therapist has left several messages on my answer phone, but I press delete without listening to them.

II

Each unkind word drives a kerf in my heart until it splinters, shards and slivers breaking off, dropping from my fingertips like crumbs onto the path below and behind me.

Crows caw in my wake, gobbling them up and I'm glad – for now there's no way back.

III

You will be the first man in six generations not to farm your family's land.

Instead you move into the winter cabin, where you bury the guilt,

ignore the looks people in the nearby village give you,

and create a different kind of legacy –

one of brushstrokes,

and pen strokes;

one of art.

IV

You hug me so tight,

arms deceptive like ivy;

a healthy tree dies.

*

V

I accouter my body in a dense black blanket and curl up at the foot of

The Old Tree.

Dead leaves and rain fall, forming a protective mulch.

Throughout the winter months, I relive all my past lives until spring

sunshine permeates, and I am, once again, reborn.

Stars

I

Standing in my mum's kitchen on Christmas Eve, Jake doesn't look like a world-famous singer.

'Hey, you,' I say.

He takes my hand, leads me to the low wall at the bottom of the garden where we sit, our heads tilted up at the tired night sky.

'Cathy–'

'Don't,' I say.

There was no break-up sex, or final kiss, nor were empty promises made; only goodbye, with the understanding that our worlds no longer aligned.

A smattering of light masquerades as a meteor shower, but I blink and it morphs into a plane, travelling far from here, lights flashing.

II

Every morning, on the 8:04, I look for her face. Sometimes I see individual stars, but never the entire constellation.

This is her train.

The train that took her face, her glorious face, and scattered her stars into darkness.

III

Every day

at the first

sighting

of the first star

a sadness

falls over me

like the

darkness of night

remembering,

how far

away you are.

IV

He handed her a star-shaped locket with a sunshine-yellow curl coiled inside. 'To remember her by,' he said.

She never wore it and the metal casing dulled, unlike the hair that should've done.

V

On our wedding night you reach into the sky and pluck me a star, place it in the bed between us. When we wake, everything is golden.

Each morning I wake to a golden sun, make golden toast for my golden family.

At night I dream in monochrome, imagine letting the colour bleed from my life.

Bleed from my perfect golden life.

Steel

I

Every May when the apple trees blush, he climbs the mountain, sits on his shadow at the summit. He remembers a different mountain, different blossoms, and a girl.

'Christopher,' she said, over-enunciating each syllable to pronounce his name properly. 'I can't.'

'Why not? I love you, you love me.'

She squeezed his hand. 'I love my family too, and they need me. Here.'

'I'll stay then.'

'No. It would never work.'

He looked at the skyscrapers in the distance and kissed her forehead.

At home he kisses his wife.

'Nice walk?' she asks, accent eroded; smooth as silk.

II

Hands, rough from years of hard labour; hands, morphed to the shapes of their tools; hands, discarded, unwanted, idle; hands, now tornadoes of boredom and rage and frustration; hands, locked together with bracelets of steel; hands that would've toiled until the life drained out of them, if they'd been allowed.

*

III

The surgeon cracks open my chest, finds my heart missing.

'I don't know why you're experiencing pain,' he tells me after. 'You can't miss what you've never had.'

IV

Memories and experiences, past and present, loop and swirl,

link up to form a chain around our necks.

Some women wear theirs with pride.

Whereas for others –

it chokes.

V

As girls' bodies develop, they are taught the flavours of life:

denial,

self-preservation,

pain,

loss.

Every generation we try to shake off the shackles,

yet teach our daughters the same.

Stone

I

When I get back from South America my mother tells me Dad is dead.

'Heart attack,' she says. 'Not surprising considering how much he ate and drank.'

'Why didn't you tell me?'

'Oh, Felicity, you'd never have got back in time. Anyway, how was your… holiday?'

'I don't want to talk about my *field trip* right now.'

'Okay, darling. Take a shower and I'll see you at dinner.'

My mother's bare feet are silent on the marble tiles as she walks away.

I drop my overweight backpack onto the floor, hear the bottle of whiskey I bought for him smash.

II

They were young, but not carefree. Never that. She the rich man's daughter; he the cook's son.

He gifted her a rose quartz pendant. She wore it every day, until she married a man "more suitable".

Once smooth, a crack now runs the length of the heart-shaped stone, splitting it apart.

III

Sun gave Earth and Moon her blessing to marry.

After a few years, Moon said she wanted more independence.

'You can't,' Earth said. 'You're nothing without me. You wouldn't even exist without me.'

Moon broke apart, floated away. She may be in pieces, but she was free.

IV

'If I've never been to a place, can I miss it?' the boy says, balancing another stone onto the jenga-jutting stack.

Bernie, his slate-coloured dog, tilts his head, sighs.

'Yes,' the boy says. 'I thought so too.'

He places a small pebble on the summit of his construction, watches it wobble, and fall.

V

I put my stone on the table for Show & Tell. 'For keeping safe,' I say.

None of the faces staring at me look like mine.

Baba told me to hold it if I was scared. When bombs fell, or Mama cried because we were hungry, I clung to my stone.

This new country, this new school, is scary.

Later that day, Miss Clark is teaching us about Stonehenge.

The girl sitting next to me smiles. 'Like the stones,' she says, pointing at the gap between her teeth. 'Like both of us.'

Not so different, after all; our friendship cemented.

About the author

Laura Besley is the author of micro fiction collection, *100neHundred* (Arachne Press, 2021), and flash fiction collection, *The Almost Mothers* (Dahlia Books, 2020).

She has been listed by TSS Publishing as one of the top 50 British and Irish Flash Fiction writers. Her work has been nominated for Best Micro Fiction and her story, To Cut a Long Story Short, will appear in the Best Small Fiction anthology in 2021. Having lived in the Netherlands, Germany and Hong Kong, she now lives in land-locked central England and misses the sea. She tweets @laurabesley

Praise for the Author

"*(Un)Natural Elements* is an exquisite jewel of a book. This collection of 45 microfiction stories is separated into nine sections, featuring five different stories in each section. And what incredible stories they are! Each one shimmers with such finely crafted language you're tempted to believe these are poems. They are not. They're beautiful little stories created by a writer at the top of her game. Laura Besley is a glistening star destined for literary glory. No doubt about it!"

- **Laura Stamps; author of *It's All About the Ride: Cat Mania*.**

"Laura Besley's collection, *(Un) Natural Elements* presents snippets of life with a dash of absurdity, sadness, matter-of-factness and humour. There are also undertones of the sinister, the fantastical and twists that come out of nowhere. If you want to read stories by someone who captures the utter complexities of being human, you should read Laura's work. Sometimes we are lovers, sometimes we are broken, sometimes we are accepting, sometimes we surprise, sometimes we are vengeful – and Laura sets out all of it on the page like a master with a succinctness I greatly admire."

- **Nikki Dudley, Streetcake editor, author and poet.**

"In (Un)Natural Elements, Laura Besley dazzles readers at the juncture of prose and poetry. A study in microfiction at its best, this collection is unflinching and memorable. Besley draws on sensory details: vinegar-drenched chips, sea salt and overdone steak juxtaposed against salt-of-the-earth characters and often-salty writing. Her microfiction explores motherhood, relationships, loss, pain, joy and regret in small pieces that are easier to swallow, and bear. From therapy to snowmen, to suckling bird babies, Besley offers us nature as mother and a mother's nature, all with the nuance and reflection of her previous collections."
- **Amy Barnes; author of *Mother Figures*.**

Manufactured by Amazon.ca
Bolton, ON

21699649R00030